MONSTROUS MYTHS

Terrible Tales of
NATIVE AMERICA

Clare Hibbert

Gareth Stevens
Publishing

Please visit our website, www.garethstevens.com. For a free color catalog of all our high-quality books, call toll free 1-800-542-2595 or fax 1-877-542-2596.

Library of Congress Cataloging-in-Publication Data

Hibbert, Clare.
Terrible tales of Native America / by Clare Hibbert.
   p. cm. — (Monstrous myth)
Includes index.
ISBN 978-1-4824-3298-5 (pbk.)
ISBN 978-1-4824-3297-8 (6-pack)
ISBN 978-1-4824-0190-5 (library binding)
1. Indians of North America — Folklore — Juvenile literature. 2. Indian mythology — North America — Juvenile literature. 3. Indians of North America — Folklore — Juvenile literature. I. Hibbert, Clare, 1970- II. Title.
E98.F6 H53 2014
398.2—dc23

First Edition

Published in 2014 by
Gareth Stevens Publishing
111 East 14th Street, Suite 349
New York, NY 10003

Copyright © 2014 Arcturus Publishing

Illustrations: Janos Jantner (Beehive Illustration)
Editor: Joe Harris
Designer: Emma Randall
Cover designer: Emma Randall

Printed in the United States of America

CPSIA compliance information: Batch #CW14GS: For further information contact Gareth Stevens, New York, New York at 1-800-542-2595.

CONTENTS

NATIVE AMERICAN STORIES

Welcome to a land of sneaky shape-changers, talking animals, terrifying monsters, and earth-shaking battles. Welcome to the weird and wonderful world of Native American mythology!

For thousands of years, the first peoples of North America lived without contact with the outside world. They didn't have presidents, churches, or libraries. But they did have chiefs, sweat lodges, and a brilliant tradition of storytelling.

There was no reading and no books, but that didn't stop Native Americans enjoying fantastic stories. Many myths were about the spirit world. Whatever their tribe, everyone believed in spirits. Native Americans thought there was a spiritual force in everything, not just people, but animals, trees, and even nonliving things like mountains and the sky!

Some tribes spent their lives on the move. It might sound like one long camping vacation, but life was tough—if the hunters had a bad day, the whole tribe went hungry. Other tribes settled in one place and farmed the land.

Native Americans loved spine-tingling stories about spirits, monsters, magic, and warriors. Not all the characters in these tales were straightforward heroes or villains. Animal tricksters were a bit more complicated—and more fun to hear about.

Tricksters such as Coyote and Raven could be brave or silly, noble or naughty. Sometimes, they were like gods and gave gifts to humankind. Other times, they were sly or downright selfish. Quite often, they got their just desserts!

A well-known Cherokee story tells how Grandmother Spider stole some of the sun to bring light to the land.

GLOOSCAP AND THE WATER MONSTER

Glooscap is a larger-than-life hero and creator spirit who turns up in many legends. As the first human, he is said to have shaped the animals, though he didn't get them all right at first! His first attempt at a squirrel was way too big—the size of a whale. It could gnaw down a tree in no time. So Glooscap remade it much smaller. He had to shrink the huge beaver and moose he made, too.

In one story, Glooscap had to face this warty water monster.

Glooscap's first attempt at a village was much more successful. His people were happy hunting, fishing, gathering plants, and collecting water. All was well until, one day, their spring ran dry. There was just a tiny dribble of slime instead of bubbling, clear water.

One poor villager was given the job of going up the valley to find out what the problem was. He passed a village of weird, web-footed people along the way. Their section of stream had a little more water, but it was stinky and horrid. So the man walked on. The sight in the next valley horrified him. A vile monster with a bloated, slimy body was blocking the source of the water.

Something tells me that this gross monster won't really care about people downstream dying of thirst.

His knees knocking, the man politely asked the monster to stop hogging all the water. "Shut up and shove off, or I'll swallow you up," croaked the beast. And to show this wasn't an empty threat, the monster opened its mouth to reveal the rotting remains of its previous victims inside. Gross!

The terrified villager ran all the way home. When he told the people about the monster, they despaired—but they needn't have. Their creator, Glooscap, had spotted what the wicked monster was doing and was coming to the rescue! Soon, his parched people would have their spring back.

The water monster didn't stand a chance against Glooscap in full warrior mode!

With a blood-curdling war cry, Glooscap set off. At the web-footed folks' village, everyone cowered at the sight of him. Glooscap ignored them and strode on to confront the monster. The fight that followed was terrifying. The earth split open and the land burst into flames. When the monster tried to swallow him, Glooscap simply grew taller and then plunged his knife into the monster's slimy, fat belly. Amazingly, a great river gushed from the wound, and its water was crystal clear.

For good measure, Glooscap squeezed the monster in his fist and flung it into the swamp. He'd transformed the massive beast into a harmless bullfrog, with wrinkled skin, bulging eyes, and a croaking voice.

Believe it or not!

Many tales describe Glooscap as a boaster. In one, he tells a woman that there's nothing he can't subdue. Giants, magicians, goblins, and witches…he's conquered them all. The wise woman simply hands Glooscap a baby, whose howls soon send him running!

THE GREAT THUNDERBIRD

The Sioux tell tales of mighty creatures called thunderbirds, which live on a mountaintop in the sacred Black Hills. These awe-inspiring animals can bring thunder with one flap of their wings, and they shoot lightning bolts from their eyes. It's just as well they're good, not evil!

The mysterious Great Thunderbird is usually cloaked in clouds.

Four paths lead up to the thunderbirds' village, where the four oldest, wisest thunderbirds live in their tepees. They are the yellow Thunderbird of the East, the red Thunderbird of the North, the bluish-white Thunderbird of the South and, most important of all, the Great Thunderbird of the West, who is black in color. Inside his tepee is a nest that holds one giant egg. That's no ordinary egg—it's the one from which all the little baby thunderbirds hatch.

Apparently a butterfly guards the east path up to the thunderbirds' village, and a bear guards the west path. I know which one I'd rather take on!

Mostly, the thunderbirds keep to themselves. However, when the wicked water monster Unktehi tried to wipe out humankind, they had to step in. The Unktehi was a bizarre-looking beast, long and scaly like a snake but with huge horns on her head. She was also enormous, filling up the entire length of the Missouri River.

By puffing up her body, the Unktehi made the Missouri flood the plains. All the smaller water monsters—her children—caused the same problem in all the smaller waterways. Thousands of people were drowned and just a handful managed to scramble to the safety of higher ground.

Great Thunderbird came down to do battle with the Unktehi while the smaller thunderbirds fought the smaller water monsters. The battle went on for years and years, but finally Great Thunderbird had to admit that his side was losing. The thunderbirds returned to their village. They were determined to overcome the evil Unktehi, but they needed a plan.

In a flash of inspiration, Great Thunderbird realized that the problem was that they were fighting the Unktehi in her own territories—down on the ground and in the water. The thunderbirds' domain was the sky, so they should fight from there instead.

The horned and scaly Unktehi was a terrifying sight to behold.

All together, the thunderbirds flew up into the sky. Then, when Great Thunderbird gave the signal, they all shot lightning bolts from their eyes and flapped their wings to produce thunderclaps. The result was explosive! The earth was scorched, rivers boiled dry, and the Unktehi and all her followers burned up.

All that was left behind were the monsters' bones, which turned to rock in the badlands or were left on the dry riverbeds. The surviving humans came down from their hiding places in the mountains and began to repeople the land.

Believe it or not!

Fossil hunters have found many dinosaur skeletons in the badlands of South Dakota. Perhaps the Sioux came up with the story of the Unktehi as a way of explaining the fossils.

THE MENACE OF MAN-EAGLE

Man-Eagle was half-human, half-bird, and all bad. He soared through the skies in a magical flint shirt that protected him from harm. He would seize women in his sharp talons, carry them off to his home, and gobble them up. One day he snatched up the wife of a warrior called Son of Light. Big mistake! Son of Light wasn't going to let some oversized budgie run off with his lady.

On his way to rescue his wife, Son of Light met some spirit people who offered to help him: the Piñon Maidens, Spider Woman, and Mole. The Piñon Maidens shaped a shirt for him out of pine resin that looked just like Man-Eagle's shirt. Then Son of Light continued on with Spider Woman, who'd made herself tiny enough to perch in his ear, and Mole.

When Son of Light reached Man-Eagle's house above the clouds, he found his wife tied up and the villain fast asleep. He spotted Man-Eagle's flint shirt hanging up and quickly swapped it for the resin one.

Son of Light wanted to teach that bird-brained Man-Eagle a lesson.

14

Just then Man-Eagle woke up and put on his shirt. When Son of Light demanded his wife back, Man-Eagle challenged him to a smoking contest. He packed a long pipe with special poisonous tobacco. Luckily, quick-thinking Mole burrowed a hole from Son of Light's feet down through the earth and into the outside air. As Son of Light smoked, all the smoke was sucked down the hole. There was nowhere for Man-Eagle's smoke to escape, though. He eventually grew dizzy and lost the contest.

Man-Eagle wore a magical armored shirt made of flint arrowheads.

Man-Eagle's next challenge was an antler-breaking contest. That cheat gave Son of Light a stone antler and himself one made of dry wood. However, Spider Woman swapped the antlers just in time. Son of Light scored a second victory.

The next contest was to see who could pull up a pine tree first, roots and all. This time Mole helped the hero by gnawing through the roots of Son of Light's tree so that it slipped out of the ground easily.

Man-Eagle was in a flap by now. He suggested an eating contest, sure he'd win because he was bigger than Son of Light. Mole helped out with his tunnel-under-the-feet trick again.

Man-Eagle's final challenge for Son of Light was to walk through fire.

16

Son of Light easily put away more meat, corn, squash, and beans than Man-Eagle because it was all carried away from his body down the tunnel! However, Man-Eagle had one last challenge up his sleeve. Would he defeat Son of Light? Of course not!

Man-Eagle Barbecued in Bizarre Shirt Mix-Up

After Man-Eagle had been defeated in four fiendish contests, he challenged Son of Light to one final test of endurance—a trial by fire. Man-Eagle was sure that his magical shirt would protect him from the flames, but he was wearing the wrong shirt and the fire burned him up in seconds. Then—a miracle! Son of Light spat into the ashes and a man rose out of them. "I was spitting special medicine that Spider Woman gave me," the hero later explained. The man from the flames calls himself Eagle-Turned-into-Man. We're pleased to report that he is not the killing type!

Believe it or not!

The story of Man-Eagle was told by the Hopi people. They believed in powerful spirit beings called kachinas. Hopi uncles carved kachina dolls as gifts for their nieces.

COYOTE'S STICKY SITUATION

Coyote was a trickster. He was always trying to get something for nothing and always bragging about his successes. Mostly, he got away with his scamming and scheming, but every so often he was outwitted.

One story tells how Coyote kept stealing wheat from a farmer. Fed up, the farmer modelled a man from sticky pitch and left it "guarding" the path to his field. That night, Coyote came to steal more ears of wheat. Thinking that the pitch man was real, he asked it to let him pass and, of course, got no reply.

Most of the time, Coyote was cunning, but not always!

Rather annoyed by this rudeness, Coyote threw a punch at the man, and his fist stuck fast. Then Coyote punched with his other hand...and that stuck, too!

Silly Coyote didn't learn his lesson. He kicked with both legs, swiped with his tail, and bit with his jaws. All ended the same way—with another body part fixed in the pitch.

The farmer found Coyote the next morning. He decided to punish the thief by throwing him into a big pot of boiling water. While the water was heating, he left Coyote chained up. Just then, Grey Fox came past scavenging for food, and Coyote saw his chance. He smooth-talked Grey Fox into taking his place by pretending that the pot was full of stew.

"You can share some of my food if you take my place for just a moment!" Once Fox was in chains, Coyote ran and foolish Fox was scalded in his place.

This wasn't the first time Coyote tricked Grey Fox — and it wouldn't be the last!

COYOTE INSIDE THE GIANT

Coyote could be silly sometimes, but he was also a hero. One of his greatest exploits was rescuing the victims of a monstrous, man-eating giant. His adventure began when he met Old Woman, who warned him there was a giant nearby. Coyote boasted that he wasn't afraid of giants—though in truth he had never met one.

Coyote breezed along, whistling, and picked up a fallen branch as a weapon. Then he went into a cave—or so he thought. It was really the giant's gaping mouth! The first person he met inside the "cave" was a woman too hungry and weak to walk. She asked Coyote about his stick and he explained that he planned to club the giant over the head with it—when he eventually found him.

Coyote didn't even notice as he walked straight into the giant's mouth.

"Too late!" The woman gave a hollow laugh. "You're already in the giant's belly!"

Coyote threw away his stick and soon he met more people, all half-dead with hunger. "Hang on!" thought Coyote. "If this is the giant's belly, we needn't starve. I can cut chunks of meat off the walls with my hunting knife."

Once he'd fed everyone, Coyote thought about how to free them. He found the giant's huge beating heart and stabbed at it with his knife. When the giant opened his mouth to take his final breath, everyone ran for it. Cunning Coyote had rescued them all!

Believe it or not!

Many tribes tell tales of Coyote, including the Apache, the Crow, the Flathead, and the Nez Perce. A similar character appears in European folklore and fairy tales—the crafty fox.

WILDCAT AND GREAT RABBIT

Great Rabbit was one of the most cunning tricksters of all. He certainly outwitted Wildcat, a meanie who was determined to catch and eat him. "If I don't catch that plump rabbit," Wildcat had sworn, "then let my lovely long tail fall off!"

One day, Wildcat picked up Great Rabbit's trail and followed it for hours. At nightfall he reached a wigwam with an old chief inside. He asked the chief, who had very long ears, if he'd noticed a rabbit run past. "A rabbit? There are thousands around here!" said the chief.

Great Rabbit was a master of disguise and a magician too!

"But it's late. Why don't you share my rabbit stew and then go hunting in the morning when you've rested?" Wildcat gratefully accepted the invitation. But he woke cold and hungry. Great Rabbit had created the wigwam with its warm fire by magic. The stew was an illusion, too!

Uh oh! Maybe no one had told Wildcat about Great Rabbit's magical powers!

Wildcat was furious when he realized he'd been hoodwinked. All day he tracked Great Rabbit. That evening he reached a village. He asked the preacher, who also had very long ears, if he'd noticed a rabbit passing. "There are thousands around here!" said the preacher. "But I don't know about Great Rabbit. Ask the chief."

So Wildcat asked the grey-haired chief, who (yes, that's right!) also had very long ears. "Ah. Great Rabbit's hard to catch," sympathized the chief. "But it's late. Why don't you eat, rest, and go looking in the morning?" Wildcat accepted but—surprise, surprise!—he woke cold and hungry again. The village, the wigwam, the food, and the cozy bearskin bed had all been illusions concocted by Great Rabbit.

On the third evening, Wildcat reached a longhouse full of people. Wildcat asked the chief, who had very long ears, if he'd seen Great Rabbit. "Let's talk later, my friend," said the chief. "Sit! Rest! We are feasting and singing." Wildcat was wary, but he was also tired and hungry, so he rested at the longhouse, and joined in with a singalong.

Great Rabbit had outwitted Wildcat again! But now he only had a little magic left. For his final illusion, Great Rabbit created a magnificent ship on a lake. Not only did it have a well-armed crew of sailors...it was also filled with cannons!

The legend explains how the American bobcat got its short, stumpy tail—it was all Great Rabbit's fault!

On the deck stood the captain in a cocked hat with two fluffy plumes that looked very like...long ears! This time, Wildcat wasn't falling for it. He swam towards the ship—but then a sudden hail of bullets and cannonballs took him by surprise. Scared to death, Wildcat finally gave up his pursuit. And then something strange happened.

Dear Momma Wildcat,

You know how you told me that I must never swear? Well it turns out that I should have listened to you! I swore that I would lose my tail if I didn't kill Great Rabbit... and now it's dropped right off! I only have a short, stumpy little tail.

What a sorry tale!

Love from Wildcat

Believe it or not!

You can hear echoes of Great Rabbit in other American trickster characters, including mischievous Brer Rabbit and the cheeky cartoon star, Bugs Bunny.

THE MAIDEN'S REVENGE

Long ago, there were two girls who were the best of friends, until they fell in love with the same man. One of the girls, Yellow Corn Ear Maiden, was part-witch. She decided to use her spooky powers to get rid of her rival. One day, while they were out fetching water from the spring, Yellow Corn Ear Maiden threw a magical, rainbow-colored wheel at Blue Corn Ear Maiden, who immediately began to sprout fur and change shape!

When Blue Corn Ear Maiden tried to return to the village, the dogs drove her away. She looked like a coyote and, worse, she smelled like a coyote. Sad and alone, the enchanted girl wandered away into the woods.

The two corn maidens used to do everything together, until jealousy reared its ugly head...

Eventually, Blue Corn Ear Maiden reached a hunting lodge. There, she found some meat to eat and skins to sleep on. That evening the hunters returned, but they weren't ordinary hunters—they were spirit people. Luckily they recognized that this was no ordinary coyote and took the animal to see wise old Spider Woman.

Spider Woman used her powerful magic to release the Blue Corn Ear Maiden from the wicked enchantment. As the other spirits watched, she transformed from a coyote into a girl! She rested with the spirit people for a few days until Spider Woman said it was time for her to go home.

Back at the village, Blue Corn Ear Maiden's family were sick with worry. Spider Woman sent her home with some instructions. So long as she followed these, she'd have her revenge on Yellow Corn Ear Maiden.

What kind of girl changes her best friend into a coyote? That Yellow Corn Ear Maiden deserves whatever she gets.

Blue Corn Ear Maiden walked back to her village, leading a procession of kachinas (spirit people). Just as Spider Woman had instructed, she told her dad to give prayer sticks and offerings to the spirit people. It felt so good to be home!

Yellow Corn Ear Maiden was surprised to see her old friend again, but she was sly and pretended to be really pleased. And Blue Corn Ear Maiden was very sweet in return—just as Spider Woman had advised her to be. No one looking at the two girls would've guessed all the bad feeling bubbling beneath the surface.

Spider Woman's magic changed Yellow Corn Ear Maiden into a big, ugly bullsnake.

28

That evening, the girls went with their jugs to fetch water. Blue Corn Ear Maiden got out a strange but beautiful cup. Intrigued, Yellow Corn Ear Maiden fell right into the trap and asked if she could drink from the cup. She took a sip, but, too late, she saw that the water in the cup was rainbow-colored. Oh no!

The moment Yellow Corn Ear Maiden drank from the cup, she began to turn into a bullsnake. "Ha! That's what you get for turning me into a coyote," laughed Blue Corn Ear Maiden.

Yellow Corn Ear Maiden was miserable as a snake—she lived all alone on a diet of rats and lizards. One day she slithered into her old village and tried to approach her parents. Mistaking her for a poisonous rattlesnake, they killed her outright. It was probably for the best. After that, Yellow Corn Ear Maiden's spirit was free.

Believe it or not!

The Hopi people believed that when any living thing died, its spirit was set free and could go to the Skeleton House—the realm of the dead.

GLOSSARY

badlands Dry, rocky land where no plants grow.

chief The most important man in a tribe.

flint A hard, grey rock that can be shaped to make a primitive tool or weapon.

fossil The remains of an animal or plant that died long ago and has been preserved in rock.

kachina A spirit being or ancestor.

kachina doll A carved wooden figure that represents a spirit being.

longhouse A traditional dwelling among some Native American tribes, shared by many families.

piñon A species of pine tree native to the American Southwest. Its wood has a distinctive smell when burned and was used in Native American ceremonies.

pitch A dark, sticky substance that hardens when it cools.

plume A long, soft feather worn in a hat as decoration.

resin A sticky, flammable substance produced by some trees.

scalplock A long lock or plait of hair left on a shaved head by some Native American men.

spirit world A realm that exists alongside the ordinary world and is inhabited by spirits.

sweat lodge A Native American hut, filled with steam created by pouring water onto hot stones, used for special rituals.

tepee A Native American tent constructed from a cone-shaped framework of poles covered with skins.

tribe A community of Native Americans who speak the same language and have close family ties. Until the coming of the European settlers, there were hundreds of tribes all over North America.

trickster A character who cheats or deceives others. Coyote and Great Rabbit were two tricksters in Native American stories.

war cry A call made by someone going into battle.

warpaint Makeup traditionally used by Native Americans to decorate their face and body before battle.

wigwam A Native American dwelling constructed from a round framework of poles covered with skins, bark, or rushes.

FURTHER INFORMATION

Further Reading

North American Indian by David Hamilton Murdoch (Dorling Kindersley, 2005)

Native American Mythology A to Z by Patricia Ann Lynch and Jeremy Roberts (Chelsea House Publishers, 2010)

Native American Myths by Neil Morris (Skyview Books, 2009)

Spider Spins a Story: Fourteen Legends from Native America by Jill Max (Rowman and Littlefield, 2007)

Websites

americanfolklore.net/folklore/native-american-myths/
Includes retellings of many famous Native American myths and legends.

nmai.si.edu/home/
The website of the National Museum of the American Indian, New York City, USA.

www.apples4theteacher.com/native-american/short-stories
Printable Native American stories.

www.indigenouspeople.net/coyote.htm
A comprehensive selection of stories about the trickster, Coyote.

www.native-languages.org/kids
Lots of resources for finding out more about Native Americans.

INDEX